The New Tax Law
How to Make it Work for You and Your Business

Edward A. Lyon JD

The New Tax Law: How to Make it Work for You and Your Business

Copyright © 2018 by Financial Gravity Companies, Inc.

All rights reserved. No part of this book may be reproduced or transmitted in any form or by any means without written permission from the author.

ISBN-13: 978-1983944161
ISBN-10: 1983944165

DEDICATION

This book is dedicated to the TaxCoach and Financial Gravity professionals who understand it's what you *keep* that counts.

CONTENTS

INTRODUCTION

Are you satisfied with the taxes you pay?

Are you confident you're taking advantage of every available break?

Are your tax and investment advisors giving you proactive advice for saving on your taxes?

If you're like most people, your answers are "no," "no," and "huh?"

And if that's the case, I've got bad news and I've got good news.

The bad news is, you're right. You probably *do* pay too much tax — maybe thousands more per year than the law requires.

You're almost certainly *not* taking advantage of every tax break you can. Our tax code is thousands of pages long, with thousands more pages of regulations. There are thousands *more* pages of IRS guidance, along with volumes of court cases interpreting all those laws, regulations, and guidance. There's no one alive taking advantage of *every* tax break they're entitled to, just because there are so many.

And most tax advisors aren't very proactive when it comes to saving their clients' money. They put the "right" numbers in the "right" boxes on the "right forms," and get them filed by the "right" deadlines. But then they call it a day. They do a perfectly fine job recording the history you give them. But wouldn't you prefer someone to help you *write* your future history?

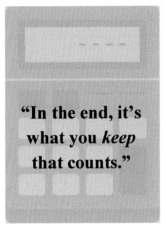

"In the end, it's what you *keep* that counts."

The good news is that you don't have to feel that way. You just need a better plan. In this book, we're going to talk about the Tax Cuts and Jobs Act of 2017, and how you can take advantage of those new rules to keep more of your what you make. In the end, it's what you *keep* that counts.

Obviously, we're not going to cover *everything* in the new law. It's full of obscure rules on topics like expensing costs for replanting citrus plants, limits on FDIC premiums that banks with more than $10 billion in assets can deduct, and net operating losses for life insurance companies. (Hopefully the size of this book was your first clue that we weren't going to squander time on those sorts of changes!)

Having said that, we're not just going to walk through the new rules here. We're going to go a step further and tell you how to take advantage of the most powerful strategy for paying less. And that strategy is *planning, proactive planning* (not the reactive planning most people do now, which doesn't work).

We call it **Strategic Tax Planning**.

#1 MISTAKE: FAILING TO PLAN

"There is nothing wrong with a strategy to avoid the payment of taxes. The Internal Revenue Code doesn't prevent that."
- Chief Justice William H. Rehnquist

The biggest mistake that most people make when it comes to taxes is failing to plan.

I don't care how good you and your tax preparer are with a stack of receipts on April 15. If you run your own business, and you didn't know you could use a medical expense reimbursement plan to write off your kid's braces as a business expense, there's nothing you can do if you haven't set up the plan!

That rule is just as true when it comes to this new tax law. If you run your own business, and you didn't know how to structure your salary to maximize the new qualified business income deduction, it's too late to fix that problem!

Right now, somewhere in America, someone is teaching a bunch of accountants how to "do taxes" under the new rules. And that's fine: "doing taxes" is just as important now as it was before the new law.

But let me ask you this. What do you *really* want from your tax professional? Do you just want to know how much you'll owe? Or would you rather know how to pay *less*?

Strategic Tax Planning means *looking forward* to minimize your taxes, not just recording history. What should you do? When should you do it? How should you do it?

And Strategic Tax Planning gives you two more powerful benefits.

"Do you just want to know how much you'll owe? Or would you rather know how to pay *less*?"

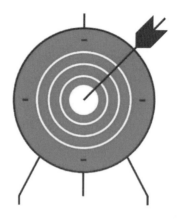

WHY STRATEGIC TAX PLANNING?

First, it's the key to your financial *defense*. You have two ways to put cash in your pocket. Financial *offense* means making more. Financial *defense* means spending less. For many of us, taxes are our biggest expense. So it makes sense to focus our financial defense where we spend the most. Sure, you can save 15% on car insurance by switching to GEICO. (Everybody knows that!) But how much will that *really* save in the long run?

And **second, Strategic Tax Planning *guarantees* results**. You can spend all sorts of time, effort, and money promoting your business or chasing *Money* magazine's latest "10 Hot Funds to Buy Right Now!" on your portfolio. But that can't guarantee results. Or you can dump your mutual funds, find a tax-efficient separate account manager, and guarantee more tax efficiency.

"**Financial *offense* means making more. Financial *defense* means spending less.**"

Are you a football fan? If so, you've probably heard the saying "offense sells tickets; defense wins games." If you're a golfer, you've heard "drive for show, putt for dough." Planning is the tax equivalent of defense winning games, and putting for dough.

THE VIEW FROM 30,000 FEET

The Tax Cuts and Jobs Act is the biggest and most important new tax law in 31 years. And while it may look like 503 pages of gobbledygook to *you*, believe it or not there's at least *some* small reason behind all that rhyme.

The law's main focus is on cutting corporate tax rates. Our old maximum corporate rate of 35% really was one of the highest in the world, and Congress thought it made us less competitive abroad. The obvious answer is to lower rates to attract business and investment here.

That's not just partisan rhetoric, either. It's true that the act passed Congress on an almost straight party-line vote. But plenty of

Democrats support corporate tax reform. Even former President Barack Obama supported cutting the top corporate tax rate down to 28%. That's not as far as the new law goes, but his support for lower rates shows that corporate tax reform really is a legitimate bipartisan goal.

Of course, not all businesses operate as taxable corporations. So Congress also wanted to cut taxes on business income that's not taxed at the corporate level. Over 90% of America's businesses are pass-through entities, and most economists will tell you that growing private businesses create more new jobs than mature, publicly-traded companies. Also, cutting corporate tax rates, without cutting pass-through individual rates, would distort the economy by pushing business owners to reorganize their entities just for the tax breaks.

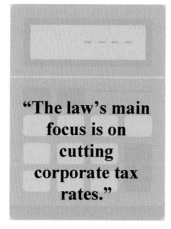

"The law's main focus is on cutting corporate tax rates."

Finally, the lawmakers wanted to lower tax rates overall. They understood it would be politically unpalatable to cut rates for the Fortune 500 without doing something for the people who work for them.

Here's the problem. Cutting all those taxes costs money. So Congress had to come up with "payfors" to make up for most (but not all) of that lost revenue. (The 2018 budget resolution let them grow the deficit by $1.5 trillion over the next 10 years.)

They did it in two ways. First, they tightened or eliminated many of the deductions we've come to take for granted over the years: personal exemptions, state and local taxes, mortgage interest, and the like.

Second, they scheduled most of the new rules for individuals to expire at the end of 2025. We'll talk more about this when we discuss new rules for individuals in Chapter Three.

So here's the bottom line: a big, unwieldy grab-bag of business and individual changes, tied together by an artificial budget target, with various phase-ins and phase outs, sprawling out over the next decade or so. OK, maybe "503 pages of gobbledygook" might not be *so* far off the mark.

HOW THE TAX SYSTEM WORKS

Let's start by taking a look at how the tax system worked *before* the new law. That will lay down a foundation for discussing where the new law changes those rules.

How The Tax System Works

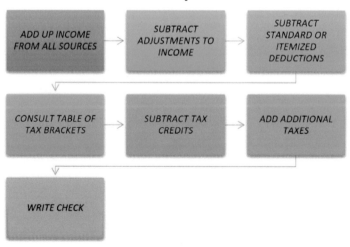

The process starts by adding up your income from all sources to calculate "total income."

Next, you'll subtract a set of specific "adjustments to income" that are available to all taxpayers, whether you itemize or not.

Next, you'll deduct your standard deduction or total itemized deductions, whichever amount is greater.

Next, you'll consult the table of tax brackets to determine your actual tax.

Next, you'll subtract any available tax credits.

Next, you'll add any extra taxes like self-employment tax or net investment income tax.

Finally, you'll stroke a check to the IRS. If you've done a decent job with your withholding and quarterly estimates, you'll get a small refund. If you've done a *great* job, you won't owe anything *or* get anything back.

Total Income

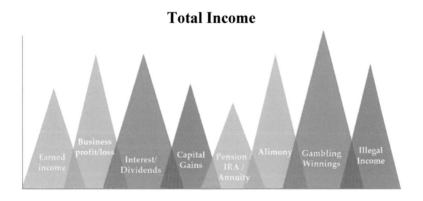

So, start with income. This includes pretty much everything you'd think the IRS is interested in:

- Earned income from wages, salaries, bonuses, and commissions,
- Profits and losses from your own business,
- Interest and dividends from bank accounts, stocks, bonds, and mutual funds,
- Capital gains from sales of investments and other property,
- Income from pensions, IRAs, and annuities,
- Alimony paid, and
- Gambling winnings.

Even illegal income is taxable. The IRS doesn't care how you make it; they just want their share! (Remember who got Al Capone!) The good news is, if you're operating an illegal business, you can deduct the same expenses as if you were running a legitimate business. So, if you're a bookie, you can deduct the cost of the cell phone you use to take bets. If you're a bank robber, you can write off your getaway car, using the actual expense or mileage allowance method.

Add all of these up, and you have Total Income.

Adjustments To Income: 2017

Once you've added up total income, it's time to start subtracting "adjustments to income." These are a group of special deductions, listed on the first page of Form 1040, that you can take whether you itemize deductions or not. Total income minus adjustments to income equals "adjusted gross income" or "AGI."

Specific adjustments include:

- IRA contributions,
- moving expenses for work-related moves,
- half of your self-employment tax, self-employed health insurance,
- self-employed retirement plan contributions,
- alimony you pay,
- "educator expenses" (up to $250 for classroom supplies that teachers pay for out of their own pockets, because society does *such* a good job of rewarding them for their contributions), and
- student loan interest.

Adjustments to income are also called "above the line" deductions, because you take them "above" the line that separates total income from AGI. That figure is important for two reasons. First, personal exemptions and itemized deductions have traditionally phased out as your AGI tops certain thresholds. (For 2017, that amount was $261,500 for single filers and $313,800 for joint filers.) Exemptions shrank by 2% for each $2,500 of income above the threshold. Deductions (except for medical expenses, investment interest, casualty and theft losses, and gambling losses) were reduced by 3% of your AGI above the threshold, up to a maximum of 80% of your total.

Second, many deductions are allowed only to the extent they exceed a certain percentage of AGI. Medical expenses were deductible only to the extent they exceeded 10% of AGI; casualty and theft losses were deductible only to the extent they exceed $100 plus 10% of AGI; and most miscellaneous deductions are allowed only to the extent they exceed 2% of AGI.

Standard Or Itemized Deductions?

MEDICAL/DENTAL EXPENSES

STATE/LOCAL TAXES

FOREIGN TAXES

INTEREST

CASUALTY/THEFT LOSSES

CHARITABLE GIFTS

MISCELLANEOUS

STANDARD DEDUCTION- 2017	
Single	$ 6,350
Head of Household	$ 9,350
Married/Joint	$12,700
Married/Separate	$ 6,350

Once you've determined your adjusted gross income, you can subtract a standard deduction based on your filing status *or* your total itemized deductions, whichever is greater.

The standard deduction for 2017 was $6,350 for single taxpayers, $9,350 for heads of households, $12,700 for joint filers, and $6,350 each for married couples filing separately. That's the easy way out, and standard deductions are high enough that about 2/3rds of taxpayers take those numbers and call it a day.

But the tax code also lets you choose to itemize if your total itemized deductions are greater . . . These include:

- Medical and dental expenses, to the extent they exceed 10% of your adjusted gross income,
- State and local income taxes *or* sales taxes, whichever is higher (you could track your actual sales tax, which could pay off if you bought something really expensive like a car, or you could use IRS tables developed to guesstimate your sales tax based on your overall income),
- Property taxes on your primary residence and any number of additional personal homes,
- Foreign taxes you pay on business or investment income,
- Mortgage interest you pay on up to $1 million of "acquisition indebtedness" on your primary home plus one additional home,
- Home equity interest you pay on up to $100,000 of home equity debt not used to improve your primary residence,
- Casualty and theft losses (to the extent they exceed $100 plus 10% of your adjusted gross income),
- Charitable gifts, and
- Miscellaneous itemized deductions like unreimbursed employee business expenses, tax preparation fees, investment

expenses, and gambling losses.

For 2017, you could also take a personal exemption of $4,050 for yourself, your spouse, and each dependent.

If your income gets too high, you start losing your itemized deductions and personal exemptions. For 2017, you lost three cents out of every dollar of itemized deduction for every dollar that your income topped $261,500 for single filers and $313,800 for joint filers, up to a maximum "haircut" of 80% of itemized deductions.

Tax deductions reduce your taxable income. If you're in the 15% bracket, an extra dollar of deductions cuts your tax by 15 cents. If you're in the 35% bracket, that same extra dollar of deductions cuts your tax by 35 cents.

Once you've subtracted deductions and personal exemptions, you'll have taxable income. At that point, the table of tax brackets tells you how much to pay.

Tax Brackets: 2017

Rate	Single	Joint
10%	0	0
15%	9,326	18,651
25%	37,951	75,901
28%	91,901	153,101
33%	190,651	233,501
35%	416,701	416,701
39.6%	418,401	470,701

The chart above shows what tax brackets looked like in 2017. As you can see, there were seven brackets, starting at 10%, and rising to

39.6% on income over about a half a million dollars. Some people actually paid more than 39.6% if they owed self-employment tax or net investment income tax on top of regular income tax.

Rates Through History

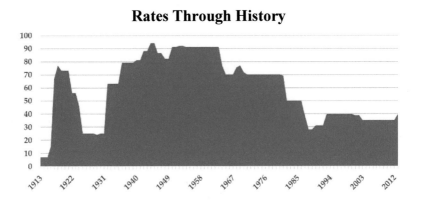

39.6% may sound like a pretty high top marginal rate, especially considering that it was just 35% until 2013. But today's rates are actually pretty low by historical standards. The very first income tax, in 1913, had a top rate of just 5% on income over $500,000 – that's about $12.6 million in today's dollars. But rates shot up quickly to pay for World War I, and went even higher to pay for World War II.

Here's some fun trivia for people who don't get out much. The Wealth Tax Act of 1935, also called the "Soak the Rich" tax, took an extra 75% of income above $5 million and hit just *one* taxpayer – Standard Oil heir John D. Rockefeller Jr.

Tax Credits

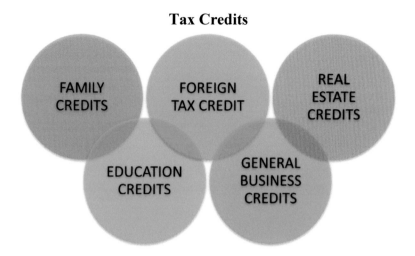

Finally, you'll subtract any available tax credits. These are dollar-for-dollar tax reductions, regardless of your tax bracket. So if you're in the 15% bracket, a dollar's worth of tax credit cuts your tax by a full dollar. If you're in the 35% bracket, an extra dollar's worth of tax credit cuts your tax by the same dollar.

There's no real secret to using tax credits, other than knowing what's out there. There are dozens available, but they fall into five main categories:

- Family credits, like the Child Tax Credit and Dependent Care Credit,
- Education credits, like the American Opportunity Credit and Lifetime Learning Credit,
- Foreign tax credits for taxes paid to foreign countries
- General business credits for all sorts of business expenses, like research & development, hiring employees from disadvantaged groups, pension plan startup expenses, and the like, and

- Real estate credits, like the low-income housing credit and renovation credit.

But Wait... There's More!

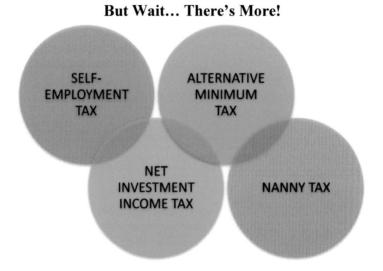

We're not done yet! As the television infomercials say, "But wait . . . There's more!"

You may also owe self-employment tax, which replaces Social Security and Medicare taxes for sole proprietors, partnerships, and LLCs.

There's also a 3.8% net investment income tax on investment income, which "Obamacare" introduced in 2013. This tax hits single taxpayers earning more than $200,000 and joint filers earning more than $250,000. For purposes of this rule, "investment income" includes interest, dividends, capital gains, rental income, royalties, and annuity distributions.

Then there's "alternative minimum tax," which requires you to throw out some of the most valuable deductions – like state and local income taxes – and recalculate your bill all over, using slightly lower rates but a bigger base. Which amount is higher, regular tax or AMT? Pay that one, thank you very much!

Finally, if you have household employees, you may have to pay a so-called "nanny tax" on their earnings. That may not sound like a big deal now. But it's definitely a big deal if you want to serve in the president's cabinet.

The bottom line here is that "tax brackets" aren't as simple as they might appear. Your *actual* tax rate can be quite a bit higher than your nominal "tax bracket."

So that's how the system worked. (Easy peasy, right?)

The system's broad outline remains the same under the new law. The real challenge isn't understanding how those rules work. The real challenge is planning to take *advantage* of those rules. How can we keep income from reaching our return in the first place? How can we create deductible employee benefit programs for our businesses? How can we make the most of adjustments to income and deductions? Where can we find more of those valuable tax credits? That's where we'll focus our attention next.

Keys To Tax Cutting

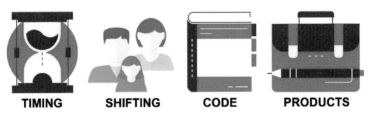

| TIMING | SHIFTING | CODE | PRODUCTS |

In the end, there are four main categories of strategies you can use to cut your tax bill:

- *Timing*–based strategies, like using a 401(k) deferrals to shift today's tax bill to tomorrow.
- Income-*shifting* strategies to move taxable income to lower-bracket taxpayers like your children.
- *Code*-based strategies, like Section 105(b) that may let you deduct your family's medical bills as a business expense, and
- *Product*-based strategies like separate-managed accounts and insurance

You'll find that most of the new law's changes fall under the code-based category.

NEW RULES FOR INDIVIDUALS

Now that we know how the tax code *used to* work, let's take a look at how the new law changes it all!

Total Income: 2018

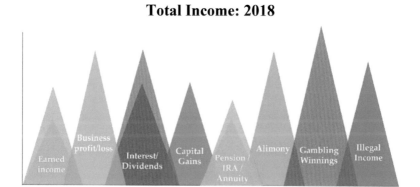

We'll start with a broad look at those different types of income.

- Earned income will be subject to new, lower rates.

- Business profit and loss may qualify for a new "qualified business income" deduction, which we'll discuss in a little bit.

- Interest and dividend income will qualify for the overall lower rates.

- Capital gains are treated the same as under the old rules.

- Retirement plan income, IRAs, and annuities are treated the same as under the old rules; however, they qualify for the new, lower rates.

- Alimony rules change big-time in 2019 – we'll talk about that when we discuss adjustments to income.

- Gambling winnings are still taxed the same as they were in 2017. And, sorry to all you would-be Bernie Madoffs, but illegal income is still as taxable as ever.

Adjustments To Income: 2018

Next, let's take a look at a couple of new rules for adjustments to income.

Moving Expenses

The deduction for moving expenses is eliminated, except for active-duty military personnel moving pursuant to a military order and incident to a permanent change of station.

Alimony

The alimony will change, starting in 2019. There won't be any effect on existing arrangements. But starting with divorce decrees, separation agreements, and modifications entered into after December 31, 2018, alimony won't be deductible by the payor or taxable to the payee. This may make divorces harder for spouses with unequal incomes because the IRS won't be subsidizing the difference between the higher-taxed and lower-taxed spouse's tax rates.

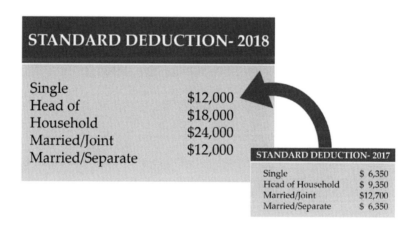

STANDARD DEDUCTION- 2018

Single	$12,000
Head of Household	$18,000
Married/Joint	$24,000
Married/Separate	$12,000

STANDARD DEDUCTION- 2017

Single	$ 6,350
Head of Household	$ 9,350
Married/Joint	$12,700
Married/Separate	$ 6,350

Once you've totaled your adjusted gross income, it's time to take your standard deduction or itemized deductions, whichever is more. And here's the first change that most people will see. Standard deductions are essentially doubling. Those amounts are already high enough that about 2/3rds of taxpayers already take them. The new rules should drop that number to about 10%.

But there's a tradeoff that may cost you big-time. Remember those $4,050 personal exemptions? They're gone now. So, let's say you're a married couple, filing jointly, with no kids. Last year, you got a $12,700 standard deduction and $8,100 in exemptions, for a total of $20,800. Suddenly that $24,000 standard deduction doesn't look *quite* so generous anymore.

If you're a married couple, filing jointly, with two kids, you got a $12,700 standard deduction plus $16,200 in exemptions, for a total of $28,900 in tax-free income. Now that $24,000 standard deduction leaves you nearly five grand in the hole compared to where you were. The lower rates and expanded child tax credit may or may not make up that difference. But you should know that doubling the standard deduction isn't quite the gift it sounds like at first.

If your deductions are still high enough to justify itemizing, then the higher standard deductions don't help you – but losing your personal exemptions will still hurt.

Itemized Deductions: 2018

MEDICAL / DENTAL EXPENSES

FOREIGN TAXES

CASUALTY / THEFT LOSSES

MISCELLANE-OUS

STATE / LOCAL TAXES

INTEREST

CHARITABLE GIFTS

Assuming it still makes sense to itemize, there are some big changes to the itemized deduction rules.

Medical/Dental Expenses

Medical and dental expenses are currently deductible only if they top 10% of your adjusted gross income. The new law lowers that threshold down to 7.5%, retroactive to January 1, 2017. However, the threshold goes back up to 10% again on January 1, 2019. So if you're going to be really sick, do yourself a favor and get it out of the way now while you can get a bigger tax advantage for it!

The lower threshold sounds nice, in theory, right? But it's really a bit of a red herring. Who wants to spend 7.5% of their income on health care? And even if you do, you only get the deduction for the part of your expenses above that threshold. Fortunately, there may be far better ways to maximize your medical deductions than hoping you have to spend enough on them to hit a 7.5% floor. If you run your own business, it's possible a medical expense reimbursement plan may let you deduct 100% of your family's medical bills as a business expense. And if you're responsible for picking your own

"there are some big changes to the itemized deduction rules."

insurance, it's possible a high-deductible insurance policy coupled with a health savings account may accomplish that same goal. There really is no reason to settle for deducting whatever portion of your medical bills tops 7.5% of your income when you can write off the whole thing.

State and Local Taxes

State and local taxes are capped at $10,000, no matter how much you actually pay. This is better than the original House of Representatives and Senate bills, which would have capped the property tax deduction at $10,000 and repealed the state and local income tax deduction entirely.

From a policy standpoint, limiting the state and local tax deduction may even change how some states raise revenue. They could grant state tax credits to encourage residents to make charitable contributions to certain funds. This would let "donors" sidestep the $10,000 limit. Or they could switch to employer-side payroll taxes or business franchise taxes, which businesses can still deduct.

Casualty Losses

The new law limits the casualty loss deduction to losses incurred as a result of a federally-declared disaster. If a meteor hits your house, but doesn't hit anyone else's house, you're going to be out of luck.

Now, there really aren't any *planning* strategies associated with this deduction, simply because nobody *plans* on getting hit by a fire or flood. That's why we buy insurance! But it's worth knowing that if you do wind up paying out of pocket for this sort of loss, the tax code won't be there to feel your pain.

Mortgage Interest

Under the old law, your deduction for mortgage interest was limited to whatever interest you paid on up to $1 million of "acquisition indebtedness" on one or more homes. You could also deduct up to $100,000 of home equity debt not used to improve your primary residence.

The new law won't change what you can deduct on existing mortgage. However, if you take out a new mortgage after December

14, 2017, the new law limits your deduction to the interest you pay on just $750,000 of debt. That figure isn't indexed for inflation, so every year the real benefit will get just a little bit smaller.

The real estate website Zillow estimates that itemizing made sense for 44% of homeowners under the old law. Under the new law, that figure will drop to around 14%.

This new, lower deduction could have some real impact on home prices, especially in urban coastal areas where prices are high. This change, coupled with lower deductions for state and local taxes, could mean a real double whammy in those areas. Some markets may see inventories fall, with fewer people choosing to move or more people choosing to renovate. This could keep prices stable. Other areas may see prices of $750,000+ homes fall, while prices of less-expensive homes actually rise.

But Congress has used the mortgage and property tax deductions to encourage homeownership for decades. In fact, this has been the prime example of using the tax code to accomplish goals indirectly rather than by legislating them directly. And it just makes sense that cutting those deductions affects the behavior that they subsidize.

The new law also eliminates the "freebie" deduction for interest on home equity debt up to $100,000, regardless of when you incurred the debt. However, home equity interest on an unlimited amount of debt is still deductible if you use the proceeds for a deductible purpose. So, if you borrow against your house to finance your business, or an investment property, you can still write it off (and ignore the $100,000 limit) as business or rental property interest.

Charitable Gifts

Under the old law, your deduction for charitable gifts of cash was limited to 50% of your adjusted gross income. If your gifts exceeded that ceiling, you could carry them forward for up to five years. The new law raises that ceiling to 60%, and keeps the five-year carryforward.

If you're a college sports fan and you make contributions in exchange for athletic seat licenses, the old law let you deduct 80% of those contributions. Now under the new law, there's no deduction for those particular donations. Rabid fans may be more interested in the seat than the deduction. But top college football programs like Alabama and Ohio State have 100,000+ tickets to sell for each home appearance. So don't be surprised if universities find new ways to license those seats.

Miscellaneous Itemized Deductions

Finally, the new law eliminates all your deductions for miscellaneous itemized deductions that were previously subject to the 2% floor. That means no more:

- unreimbursed employee business expenses,
- tax preparation fees,
- union dues,
- IRA custodial fees, and
- investment expenses.

(Honestly, if you're deducting a lot of your own money on your employee business expenses, you should consider reclassifying your relationship with your employer to become an independent contractor.

We'll talk about the specific benefits of that move in the next chapter when we discuss qualified business income.)

However, the new law preserves a different set of miscellaneous itemized deductions *not* subject to the 2% floor. These include gambling losses (up to gambling winnings), casualty and theft losses from income-producing property, federal estate tax on income in respect of a decedent, and losses from Ponzi-type schemes.

Limitation on Itemized Deductions

By now, your itemized deductions are probably looking *a lot* less valuable. Well, now there's a little good news. Remember those "Pease limits" we talked about, the ones that phase out your itemized deductions if your income tops $261,500 for single filers or $313,800 for joint filers? Now they're gone. That means that if you do still get to itemize, you'll get to use *all* those deductions instead of taking the usual haircut.

Tax Brackets: 2018

Rate	Single	Joint
10%	0	0
12%	9,526	19,051
22%	38,701	77,401
24%	82,501	165,001
33%	157,501	315,001
35%	200,001	400,001
37%	500,001	600,001

Here's the biggest change, the one that affects everyone who owes tax. Remember, back in 2017 there were seven tax brackets, starting at 10% and topping out at 39.6%. The Tax Cuts and Jobs Act keeps that seven-bracket structure, but cuts most of those rates.

Your bottom-line results here could be dramatic, or not, depending on how much you earn, how you earn it, where you spend it, and how many people you're supporting.

The changes in tax brackets are pretty obvious. But here's another important change that you won't see reflected on the chart. In 1985, Washington started indexing elements of the tax code, like standard deductions, personal exemptions, and tax brackets, so that rising inflation wouldn't push taxpayers into higher brackets.

The IRS has used the Consumer Price Index, or CPI, to measure inflation. However, the new law specifies a different index, called the "chained" consumer price index. This index assumes that as prices go up, consumers react by choosing cheaper goods. For example, if the price of apples goes up, you probably won't stop eating them – but you might switch from Golden Delicious to Granny Smith. (If you're a millennial, substitute "avocado toast" for apples, and you'll get the point.)

The bottom-line result here is that that "chained" CPI rises more slowly compared to the regular CPI. The nonpartisan Tax Policy Center estimates that changing to chained CPI would increase taxes paid by 30% of the bottom quintile of the income distribution, 70% of the next quintile, and nearly all of the taxpayers in the top 60% of income. Bottom line, switching to chained CPI will function like a small but noticeable annual, across-the-board tax hike.

Tax Credits: 2018

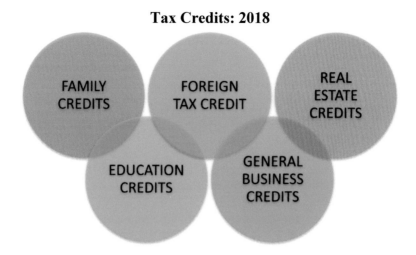

Finally, there are several changes to the tax credit rules that may affect you.

Child Tax Credit

Under the old rules, the child tax credit was capped at $1,000 per child, under age 17. The credit phased out by $50 for each $1,000 of "modified adjusted gross income" above $75,000 (single filers) or $110,000 (joint filers). (Modified adjusted gross income equals regular adjusted gross income, plus a seemingly random laundry list of items like nontaxable municipal bond interest, student loan interest, half of your self-employment tax, and any deductible college expenses.) If the credit was more than your actual tax bill, you might qualify for an "additional child tax credit" to the extent of any earned income above $3,000. (Sure makes you wish you could fill out your taxes on a postcard, right?)

The new rules double the child tax credit to $2,000 per child. They raise the threshold for phasing it out to $200,000 for single filers and $400,000 for joint filers. And they raise the refundable portion to

$1,400 and indexes that amount for inflation.

Remember when we talked about those disappearing personal exemptions? The worst-hit taxpayers are the those with children. The new child tax credit rules should restore some of those lost benefits for those particular taxpayers.

The new law also provides a new $500 nonrefundable credit for dependents other than children. The rules here for claiming the credit are generally the same as they would be for claiming someone as a dependent.

Foreign Tax Credit

Most people who take the foreign tax credit do so because they own mutual funds that pay foreign tax on international investments. At the end of the year, you get a Form 1099-DIV, and if there's an amount in Box 6, you can carry it forward to Page Two of Form 1040.

The new law makes no changes to those particular rules. However, it repeals rules that used to let you take a credit for foreign taxes paid on dividends that aren't taxed here in the U.S. There are also new anti-base erosion rules subjecting to U.S. corporate shareholders of controlled foreign corporations to tax on 50% of their "global intangible low-taxed income" (GILTI) with a deduction of 37.5% for foreign-derived intangible income. (I'll take a break now for you to get up and get an aspirin.)

Changes Here? Changes Here!

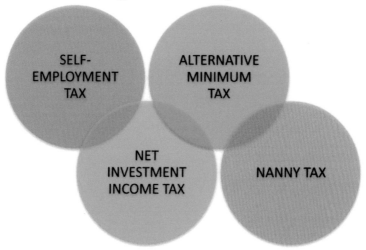

The new law doesn't make any changes to the self-employment tax rules, the net investment income tax, or that pesky nanny tax. However, it does make some changes to the hated alternative minimum tax. Specifically, it raises the exemption amount from $53,900 to $70,300 for single filers and from $83,800 to $109,400 for joint filers. It also increases the phaseout of those exemptions from $119,700 to $500,000 for single filers and from $159,700 to $1 million for joint filers. While this isn't nearly as good as eliminating the AMT, it should protect millions of filers from its reach.

It's also worth mentioning that the new law does nothing about the net investment income tax, which Congressional Republicans had previously targeted as part of Obamacare repeal efforts.

Okay, let's take a look at some case studies to see how all of these changes tie together.

Case Study: *Married With Children*

	2017	2018
Adjusted Gross Income	100,000	100,000
Standard/Itemized Deductions	12,700/24,000	24,000/22,000
Personal Exemption	16,200	0
Taxable Income	59,800	76,000
Tax Before Credits	8,038	8,739
Child Tax Credit	2,000	4,000
Total Tax	**6,038**	**4,739**

Example assumes married couple with two children under age 15, filing jointly with $12,000 in mortgage interest and $12,000 in property taxes.

The Smiths are married with 2 children, a golden retriever, and a cat. Mr. and Mrs. Smith each make $50,000 per year working boring office jobs at cubicle farms in the suburbs. They pay $12,000 per year in mortgage interest and $12,000 per year in property tax.

For 2017, they start with $100,000 in adjusted gross income. Their itemized deductions total $24,000, which is higher than the $12,700 standard deduction, so they itemize. They have $16,200 in personal exemptions. This gives them a taxable income of $59,800, a tax before credits of $8,038, and a final tax bill after the child tax credit of $6,038. They're in the 15% tax bracket, which means if one of them brings home a hundred-dollar bonus, they'll pay $15 extra dollars on that income. And their average tax rate is 6%.

Fast forward a year to 2018, and now let's see what we have. Their income starts at the same $100,000. But now, because their property tax deduction is capped at $10,000, their $22,000 of itemized deductions is actually below the $24,000 standard deduction. That's $2,000 less than in 2017. And they lose their personal exemptions entirely. That puts their taxable income at $76,000, more than $16,000 higher than in 2017.

But now their marginal tax bracket is 12%, not 15%. Their tax before credits is a little bit higher, at $8,739. But their child tax credits have doubled, leaving them a final bill of $4,739. Their marginal tax bracket is 12%, which means if one of them brings home a $100 bonus, they'll pay $12 tax on that income. And their average tax rate drops to 4.7%.

The difference between the two years is $1,299, or $3.56 per day. Yeah, it beats paying more. But nobody's going to plan on getting rich on an extra $3.56 per day.

Case Study: *Retired*

	2017	2018
Adjusted Gross Income	80,000	80,000
Standard/Itemized Deductions	12,700/12,000	24,000/10,000
Personal Exemption	8,100	0
Taxable Income	59,900	56,000
Tax Before Credits	8,052	6,339
Child Tax Credit	0	0
Total Tax	8,052	6,339

Example assumes married couple, ages 64 & 62, filing jointly with no mortgage interest and $12,000 in property taxes.

Next, we've got a retired couple enjoying their golden years. The Joneses are married with grown children and the good sense not to own pets. They draw $60,000 in pension income and $20,000 in taxable Social Security benefits from when they worked boring jobs in downtown cubicle farms. They pay $12,000 per year in property tax.

For 2017, they start with $80,000 in adjusted gross income. Their itemized deductions total $12,000, which is less than the $12,700 standard deduction, so they take the standard deduction. And they have $18,100 in personal exemptions. This gives them a taxable income of $59,900, and a tax bill of $8,052, and a final tax bill after the child tax credit of $6,038. They're in the 15% tax bracket and their average tax rate is 10.1%.

Drink a toast to 2018, and now let's see what we have. Their income starts at the same $80,000. They still don't have enough deductions to itemize, but now their standard deduction is up to $24,000. That's a nice bonus from 2017. However, they lose their $8,100 in personal exemptions. That puts their taxable income at $56,000, more than $16,000 higher than in 2017. But the 2018 tax bracket is lower, which means less tax. So their final bill is just $6,339. Their marginal bracket is 12%, which means if one of them wins $100 playing bingo, they'll pay $12 tax on that income. And their average tax rate drops to 7.9%.

The difference between the two years is $1,713, or $4.69 per day. Again, it beats paying more. But $4.69 a day isn't going to buy many rounds of golf, or even cocktails at the 19th hole. If you really want to pay less, you can't count on the new tax law to do it for you.

Changes Involving Children

We mentioned earlier that there are four main categories of ways to save taxes: timing, shifting, code, and product. The new law takes dead aim at one classic strategy, and that's shifting investment income to your children to be taxed at their lower rates.

For most of us, our children don't earn a lot of money, which puts them in a lower bracket. Let's say you have $100,000 in the bank earning $1,000 in annual interest. If you're in the 24% tax bracket, you'll pay $240 in tax on that income. But if your child is in the 0% bracket, and you put the account in their name, they'll pay nothing. Seems like an obvious strategy, right?

Well, the folks who write the tax laws aren't stupid, and they see that loophole. So they created the "kiddie tax" rules. Those rules say that if your child earns more than $2,100 in investment income, anything above that amount is taxed at your rate, not theirs. Those rules apply until your child hits age 19, or age 24 if they're a fulltime student and you claim them as a dependent. There's even an alternative minimum tax adjustment for "kiddie tax" income.

"Kiddie Tax" Penalty: 2018

Rate	Single	Trusts/Estates
10%	0	0
12%	9,526	
22%	38,701	
24%	82,501	2,551
33%	157,501	
35%	200,001	9,151
37%	500,001	12,501

The new law keeps that same concept of special rates on your child's unearned income. But now, instead of paying tax at *your* rate, they'll pay tax at special rates that apply to trusts and estates.

Why is that so bad? Well, just take a look at the rates! They *look* easier because there are just four of them. But wow, they are a *steep* climb. They start at the same 10% as for everyone else. But they jump to 24% after just $2,550 of income, then 35% after $9,150, and finally to the top 37% rate after just $12,500.

This came as a surprise for a lot of people. But it's really going to crush that particular income-shifting strategy.

While we're on the topic of children, the new law offers one nice new opportunity. If you have kids, you've probably heard of "Section 529" college savings plans, which let you contribute money to an account in the child's name and grow those assets tax-free to use for the child's college education. While there's no *federal* deduction for contribution, over 30 states offer deductions or credits for those amounts.

The new law lets you use up to $10,000 per year per account for kindergarten through high school expenses. Now, the savings here probably won't make a huge difference on your federal taxes, especially if you're using the account for a younger child. There just won't be enough time for the tax savings to add up. But it could make a really nice difference on your state tax bill if you're sending your kids to private or religious schools. It could also blunt the effect of limiting the state and local tax deduction to just $10,000 per year (by lowering the amount you actually pay, closer to the threshold or even below it).

Roth IRA "Do-Overs"

Here's a change that probably won't affect you – but if it does, you won't like it at all.

Since 2011, you've been allowed to convert your traditional IRA balance to a Roth IRA. This can make tremendous sense if the tax you pay to convert now is less than the tax you would pay to withdraw funds down the road. That's not always easy to determine! And sometimes, in hindsight, converting can be a clear mistake. Let's say you're in the 25% bracket, and you estimate that you can convert $30,000 without stepping up into the 28% bracket. But at the end of the year, you realize that $8,000 of your conversion is taxed at the higher rate. Or, worse yet, the value of your account drops and you wind up paying tax on phantom earnings.

Under current law, if you decide converting was a mistake, you can undo the conversion. It's one of the few legitimate "tax time machines" in the entire code.

And… now it's gone. Sorry, no more backsies!

Watch Out For 2026!

Now let's talk about a *big* caution to keep in mind before you get too comfortable with all these changes.

Remember the story of Cinderella? Her fairy godmother sent her to the ball to dance with the prince, but warned her to be home by midnight or her carriage would turn back into a pumpkin. Well for many of us, the Tax Cuts and Jobs Act turns into a pumpkin, too, at the stroke of midnight on December 31, 2025.

Here's the problem. Congressional Republicans knew they had to pass the new law under special "reconciliation rules" to avoid a Democratic filibuster. That meant they were subject to a Senate budget rule – the "Byrd Rule," named after longtime Democratic Senator Robert Byrd – that said they can't increase the deficit beyond 10 years.

Corporate tax cuts were their first priority – and they wanted to make those cuts permanent. They would have loved to make the personal tax cuts permanent, too. But they couldn't do that without violating the Byrd Rule. So they decided to kill the personal tax cuts after 2025.

Now, the assumption here is that the personal cuts won't *really* expire. In 2001 and 2003, the Bush administration cut rates using the same reconciliation procedures. That led to the 2012 "fiscal cliff," when tax rates were supposed to jump back to pre-2001 levels. At 12:01AM on January 1, 2013, we actually went "over the cliff." But later that day, Congress made the lower rates permanent except for single filers making over $400,000 and joint filers making over $450,000. (Congress may be stuck at around 11% approval – but one thing everyone agrees they're great at is waiting until the last possible moment to do anything important!)

The assumption now is that once we get closer to 2026, Washington will extend the lower personal rates like they extended the Bush tax cuts in 2013. Of course, anything can happen between now and then. The earth could get hit by a comet, which would make marginal tax rates pretty irrelevant (as well as solving a bunch of other problems, too).

So, we've set ourselves up for another fiscal cliff on December 31, 2025. And if history repeats itself, we'll ring in the New Year without a resolution. But let's take a quick look at what we lose if we go over that next cliff:

- Marginal rates will jump back to 2017 levels.
- Standard deductions will drop back to 2017 levels.
- AMT exemptions will drop back to 2017 levels.
- The Pease limits on itemized deductions will come roaring back.
- The AGI limits on charitable contributions will drop back to 50%.
- The child tax credit will drop back to $1,000 and start phasing out at 2017's lower thresholds.
- The estate tax unified credit drops back to the $5 million

baseline (plus regular inflation adjustments).

Of course, the 2025 fiscal cliff won't be *all* bad. That's because the 2017 Act closes a lot of deductions to pay for the overall rate cuts. Those deductions will open back up again:

- Personal exemptions will come back. (Yay!)
- Miscellaneous itemized deductions subject to the 2% floor will come back.
- The mortgage interest deduction will revert to $1 million of acquisition indebtedness, and interest on up to $100,000 of home equity debt will be deductible again.
- State and local income, sales, and property taxes will be fully deductible.
- Casualty and theft losses will be deductible, subject to the usual $100 plus 10% AGI floor, outside of federally declared disaster areas.
- Moving expenses will be deductible for non-military moves.

NEW RULES FOR BUSINESSES

Now that we've outlined how the tax system for individuals, let's talk about how it works for business entities. This is where the meat

Taxes On Business Entities

of the bill lies, and this is where you'll find the most powerful actionable strategies!

The first thing you need to know is that there are four different tax classifications for businesses: sole proprietorships, partnerships, S corporations, and C corporations.

Now, you may be looking at this list and thinking, "wait a minute… my business is a limited liability company, or LLC. Where do LLCs fall on the list?" The answer is that an LLC is a type of entity, formed under state law. But it's not a *tax* classification. LLCs can actually choose to be taxed as whatever entity they want. A single-member LLC, with just one owner, is assumed to be "disregarded," and taxed as a sole proprietorship. But that same single-member LLC can also elect to be treated as an S corporation or a C corporation. Likewise, a multiple-member LLC, with two or more owners, will be taxed as a partnership. But those owners can also elect to be taxed as an S corporation or a C corporation.

Business Taxes, Explained

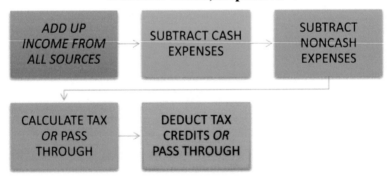

Regardless of which entity you choose, the basic process works the same.

- First, add up your income from all sources. This includes sales or service income, subscription revenue, and anything else your customers pay you throughout the year. It also includes investment income from bank accounts or investment portfolios your company owns.

- Next, subtract cash expenses, like cost of goods sold, salaries and wages, rent and office expenses, interest, employee benefits, and the like.

- Next subtract *non*cash expenses. This includes depreciation on capital assets, like real estate and equipment, that your business buys. It also includes amortization of intangible assets, like startup expenses and goodwill.

Once you have a final bottom line result, you'll either pay tax on it at the corporate level if you're taxed as a C corporation, or pass it through directly to the owners if you're taxed as a proprietorship, partnership, or S corporation. Sole proprietorships, by definition, have just one owner – so they report their income on Schedule C directly on that owner's personal return. Partnerships and S corporations give each owner a Schedule K-1 reporting their share of income and expenses.

Finally, C corporations can take tax credits directly on their own return. Proprietorships, partnerships, and S corporations use Schedule K-1 to pass those credits through to their owners, where there may be further limits.

Corporate Tax Rates: 2017

Taxable Income	Rate
0 – $50,000	15%
$50,001 – 75,000	25%
$75,001 – 100,000	34%
$100,001 – 335,000	39%
$335,001 – 10,000,000	34%
$10,000,001 – 15,000,000	35%
$15,000,001 – 18,333,333	38%
$18,333,334+	35%

- Personal Service Company
- Personal Holding Company
- Corporate AMT
- Accumulated earnings tax

For 2017, the corporate tax system had three statutory rates: 15% on the first $50,000 of income, 25% on the next $50,000, and 35% on anything above that. However, the tables phase out the benefit of the lower 15% and 25% rates as the corporation's taxable income goes up, so what we actually ended up with was a ridiculous eight-layer cake that repeated the 34% and 35% brackets twice as you moved up the ladder.

For some reason, that wasn't complicated enough. So the code offered a few more hurdles to jump:

- "Personal service corporations" engaged in accounting, actuarial science, architecture, consulting, engineering, health (including veterinary services), law, and the performing arts paid a flat 35% rate. The goal here was to keep personal service professionals from avoiding tax by leaving it inside their corporations.

- "Personal holding companies" are corporations where more than 50% of the value of the outstanding stock is owned directly or indirectly by five or fewer individuals *and* more than 60% of their income is earned from passive sources – interest, dividends, rents, royalties, annuities, mineral rights, and the like. PHCs pay a 20% penalty tax on undistributed PHC income.

- There was a 20% corporate alternative minimum tax. The goal here was the same as with the individual AMT, to make sure that profitable corporations don't use too many loopholes to skate by without paying their fair share.

- Finally, the IRS didn't want you sitting like Scrooge McDuck on giant piles of cash inside your corporation. They wanted you to distribute it as dividends and pay tax on it. So there's an accumulated earnings tax equal to 15% of whatever amount the IRS deems to be above and beyond your corporation's ordinary and reasonable business needs.

Of course, your "ordinary and reasonable business needs" is a pretty subjective standard. So the law offers a $250,000 safe harbor ($150,000 for personal service corporations). That does *not* mean that amounts above $250,000 are automatically subject to the tax. It all depends on your ability to show the IRS that you need the accumulation for your business. But amounts under that threshold won't attract any extra attention.

Corporate Tax Rates: 2018+

Taxable Income	Rate	
0 – $50,000	21%	▪ Personal Service Company
$50,001 – 75,000	21%	▪ Personal Holding Company
$75,001 – 100,000	21%	▪ Corporate AMT
$100,001 – 335,000	21%	▪ Accumulated earnings tax
$335,001 – 10,000,000	21%	
$10,000,001 – 15,000,000	21%	
$15,000,001 – 18,333,333	21%	
$18,333,334+	21%	

Under the new law, things get considerably easier. There's a single flat rate of 21% that applies from your first dollar of income to your very last dollar of income.

And there's more good news. The new law eliminates the personal service company tax and corporate AMT. If you have a credit for prior years' AMT, you can carry it forward to offset your regular tax liability.

The new rules will make C corporations far more valuable to business owners, and even investors. Consider these possibilities:

Traditional Income Shifting

Highly paid professionals who can incorporate their practice can take income in the form of salary, taxed at rates as high as 40.8% (37% for income tax plus 3.8% for Medicare tax). Alternatively, they can leave profits inside the corporation to be taxed at 21%, then take the after-tax net income as a dividend, taxed at 23.8% (20% for income tax on qualified corporate dividends and 3.8% net investment income tax). Together, this will result in a 39.802% rate.

Qualified Plan Alternative

You can also use a C corporation as an alternative to a qualified retirement plan. Simply leave earnings in the corporation (to be taxed at the regular 21% corporate rate) and withdraw them as dividends in a later year when you're in a lower tax bracket.

Stepped-Up Basis Shelter

If you're nearing the end of your career, and don't need the income you're earning from your business for current living expenses, consider parking them inside your C corporation until your death. At that point, your heirs will enjoy a "stepped-up basis" on those assets, which means they can withdraw the accumulated funds tax-free.

A New Kind Of Income

| Ordinary | Investment | Passive | Qualified Business |

Now let's talk about the new law's biggest change for most business owners: a new kind of income from pass-through businesses.

The tax code has always recognized that there are different kinds of income – and treated those kinds of income differently.

Ordinary income is what you earn from your work or your business. If you earn a salary from a job, and your spouse loses money in a business, you can net those amounts against each other. If you draw pension or IRA income, that's ordinary income too. Ordinary income is taxed at ordinary rates.

Investment income is income you earn from your portfolio. And some of it, like taxable interest income, is taxed at ordinary income rates. But different kinds of investment income can be taxed at different rates. Qualified corporate dividends, for example, are taxed at special rates and capped at 20%. Long-term capital gains from property held for more than a year are also capped at 20%. And investment income is subject to a 3.8% "net investment income tax" if your AGI exceeds $200,000 for single filers or $250,000 for joint filers.

Now, if you have capital losses in a year, you can subtract them from your capital gains. And you can subtract up to $3,000 of net capital losses against your ordinary income. But if your net capital loss is more than $3,000, you have to carry the remainder forward to future years. So, for the most part, investment income is walled off into its own little silo.

By the mid-1980s, taxpayers had figured a way around that wall. They discovered they could use borrowed money to increase their basis in investments like real estate, oil & gas, and equipment leasing, and write off huge paper losses, well in excess of what they had actually invested. They used those losses to offset their ordinary income from salaries and businesses, as well as investment income from their investment portfolios. That was great for taxpayers, of course, especially with marginal rates hitting 70%. But it wasn't so good for the U.S. Treasury.

So, in 1986, Congress created a new category of income, called passive income, from activities where you don't "materially participate." The 1986 rules said that you can write off passive losses against passive income – but generally not against ordinary income or investment income. There's a rental real estate loss allowance for up to $25,000 of rental property losses, but that phases out starting to $100,000 of adjusted gross income. And so-called "real estate professionals" who qualify under special rules can deduct passive real estate losses against ordinary income. But for the most part, the 1986 rules walled off passive income and losses into their own silo.

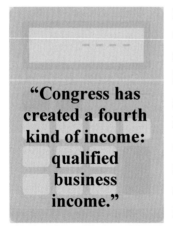

"Congress has created a fourth kind of income: qualified business income."

Now Congress has created a fourth kind of income: qualified business income. Here's why they needed to do that. The new tax law lowered the top tax on C corporation income from 35% to 21%. That's a whole lot less than the maximum 37% tax on pass-through income from sole proprietorships, partnerships, and S corporations. To equalize the tax treatment between taxable and pass-through businesses, the Act creates a new category of income called "qualified business income" (QBI) and lets you deduct 20% of that income, calculated on an activity-by-activity basis, from your taxable income for the year.

Qualified Business Income

QBI includes net business income from sole proprietorships, partnerships, and S corporations. It also includes pass-through income from real estate investment trusts, publicly-traded partnerships, and qualified agricultural coops. But it doesn't guaranteed payments or W2 wages you draw from your business. It also doesn't include investment income: most taxable dividends other than REITs, or coops, investment interest income, short-term or long-term capital gains, commodity or foreign currency gains, etc.

However, there are three important limits to this new deduction.

First, if your 2018 taxable income – *after* adjustments to income and itemized deductions -- is over $157,500 ($315,000 for joint filers) your QBI deduction for each activity is limited to the greater of:

- 50% of the W2 wages timely paid on behalf of that activity, *or*
- 25% of the W2 wages plus 2.5% of the initial cost, immediately after acquisition, of all tangible property placed in service on behalf of that activity. (Tangible property includes real estate, equipment and machinery, vehicles, or robots that replace your employees.) You can count the initial cost property towards this amount for 10 years

Example: You own 20% of an S corporation that pays $500,000 in W2 wages and has $200,000 of property in service. Your QBI is the greater of $50,000 (50% of your 20% share of $500,000 in wages) or $26,000 (25% of your 20% share of $500,000 in wages plus 2.5% of your 20% share of the $200,000 in depreciable property).

Second, if your QBI comes from a "specified service business" (medicine, law, accounting, actuarial science, financial services, consulting, performing arts, athletics, or any business that relies on the "reputation or skill of one or more employees"), your deduction for that activity phases out as your taxable income rises from $157,500-207,500 (single filers) or $315,000-415,000 (joint filers).

Third, the overall QBI deduction is limited to 20% of your taxable income in any particular year. There's no provision for carrying over any unused deduction. However, if your QBI for the year is below zero, you can carry the loss forward to the next taxable year.

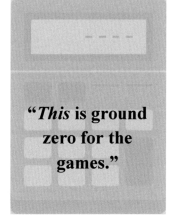

"*This* is ground zero for the games."

The new rules suggest several ways to maximize the new benefit. And honestly, the more time tax lawyers and accountants spend looking over these rules, the more ideas they'll come up with. When critics of the tax bill say it will encourage "gaming the system," *this* is the provision they're talking about. *This* is ground zero for the games.

Create W2 Income

If you currently operate a non-service business as a sole proprietor or partner, you have few or no W2 employees, and your taxable income is above the $157,500/$315,000 threshold, consider establishing an S corporation and paying yourself a W2 wage to create a base for taking advantage of the deduction.

"Cracking and Packing"

Consider "cracking and packing" strategies to avoid the $157,500/$315,000 limits on specified service income.

If your primary activity is a specified personal service, consider "cracking" out ancillary activities, like marketing or management, into a separate activity. You'll still lose out on the deduction for that primary service activity, but you'll preserve the deduction for the ancillary activities that don't fall under the service business definition.

Alternatively, if part of your income comes from services, but a significant portion comes from elsewhere, you could "pack" non-service activities into a single entity so that it's *not* primarily providing services – and in that way, sidestep the service business limits.

Side Income

If you earn income from a side gig, consider segregating it into a separate activity. Let's say you throw passes for a pro football team. You probably also make income from endorsements. Your football salary won't qualify for the QBI deduction. But you can segregate your endorsement earnings into a separate entity to take advantage of the QBI deduction.

It's true that someday the IRS or Tax Court may rule that endorsements are a "specified service business" because they rely on "the reputation or skill of one or more employees." But why would you jump the gun and make that determination for them?

Segregate Real Estate

If you own real estate for your business to occupy, consider separating that real estate into a separate entity and paying it the highest reasonable rent to qualify for the deduction.

Ideally, you'll do this in the form of a real estate investment trust (REIT), because REIT pass-through dividends automatically qualify as QBI, no matter how much the REIT pays in W2 wages.

REITS have to have 100 shareholders. However, we can help you find 100 preferred shareholders to invest $1,000 each in exchange for a $100 annual dividend. This gives them a sweet 10% return on their investment. And it lets you qualify for the attractive REIT tax treatment for a minimal $10,000 per year cost.

Contractors to Employees

If your business utilizes independent contractors, consider making them W2 employees to maximize the W2 base for calculating the QBI deduction. (Of course, if those contractors are *also* paying attention to the law, they may prefer to *keep* that status!)

Quit Your Job!

If you're working for the man, waking up to the noise of the alarm and trudging off to work every day to collect your pay, you're probably a little bit envious of your self-employed peers. They really could be doing the exact same work as you and paying tax on 20% less income, just because they run their own business.

So don't get mad, get even. "Quit" your job and join them!

Seriously, is there a way to renegotiate your relationship with your employer to become an independent contractor? If so, you'll immediately recharacterize your income in a way to take advantage of the new rules . . . as well as all the other planning opportunities available to business owners.

If you do find yourself able to renegotiate your relationship with your (soon-to-be-former) employer, be sure not to blow it when negotiating your pay. Don't just settle for your old salary – remember that your employer is also paying their half of your social security tax, and may be paying even more for healthcare coverage, retirement plan contributions, expense reimbursements, and other nontaxable benefits.

Final Notes on QBI

I realize this is going to sound self-serving. But this really isn't "do-it-yourself" planning. Just because you can buy a tool to do something yourself – instead of hiring a professional to use the tool – doesn't mean you should. If you go to Amazon.com and search for "orthopedic bone saw," you can find them for under twenty bucks. (Take a look. Seriously, it's terrifying!) But just because you can buy the tool cheap, it doesn't mean you should be setting your kids' broken bones!

Want to hear something funny? Here's what the congressional conference committee responsible for final text of the Qualified Business Income provisions said in their report:

> *"It is not anticipated that individuals will need to keep additional records due to the provision. It should not result in an increase in disputes with the IRS, nor will regulatory guidance be necessary to implement this decision."*

Ha! Do you think they actually believe that? Or is it just something they told themselves to feel better about unleashing a hurricane of new uncertainty into the system?

Depreciation & Expensing

Now let's walk through some specific business deductions. We'll start with depreciation and expensing.

Here's the basic concept. Traditionally, when you buy something durable, like a building, or a truck, or machinery for your business, you don't get to just deduct it right away. You have to deduct it over time, a period of time that approximates the useful life of the property. This process is called 'depreciation."

To depreciate property, the first thing you need to know is your "basis." This usually just means how much it costs.

The next thing you need to know is the "recovery period," or "life." Most machinery and equipment is "five-year property" or "seven-year property," which means you write it off over five years or seven years. Land improvements, like driveways and parking lots, are generally 15-year property. Residential real estate depreciates over 27.5 years. And finally, nonresidential real estate depreciates over 39 years.

The next thing you need to know is what "method" to use. Some property depreciates over a straight line. With real estate, for example, you divide the basis by the recovery period – 27.5 years for residential property or 39 years for nonresidential property. If you buy an office condominium for $390,000, you'll deduct $10,000 per year. But most property qualifies for some form of "accelerated depreciation," which lets you write off more in the early years. There's the 200% declining balance, the 150% declining balance, and some property switches from one method to another once you reach a certain point. Trust me, we don't need to go into any more detail than that.

Finally, you'll need to know which "convention" to use. The rationale here is that, unless you buy something on January 1, you shouldn't get to deduct an entire year's worth of depreciation that year. So there's the half-year convention, the mid-quarter convention, and the mid-month convention, depending on what you're buying.

Does this all make your head hurt? You know who else's heads hurt? The accountants who work for the companies that buy all this stuff and have to make smart decisions about when to buy it!

Now let's throw in a couple more complications.

First, sometimes the tax code lets you take "bonus depreciation" the year you buy something. For example, if you bought a car for your business between September 8, 2010, and January 1, 2014, you could deduct an extra $8,000 the year you bought it. If you bought equipment, you could deduct 50% off the top, and depreciate the remaining 50% over the usual recovery period using the usual method and usual convention.

Second, the law lets some property qualify for "first year expensing," which lets you deduct it outright rather than depreciating over time. For 2017, you could expense up to $500,000 of tangible personal property, new or used, except for most passenger vehicles. That deduction phased out by one dollar for every dollar of qualifying property placed in service during the year that topped $2.0 million.

"trust me when I say that this is a big deal."

Why complicate things with bonus depreciation and first-year expensing? Well, the goal here is to stimulate the economy by making it easier for businesses to buy equipment and grow. And now you've probably figured out why we're walking through all of these rules.

The Tax Cuts and Jobs Act lets you take 100% bonus depreciation on any qualified property you place in service after September 27, 2017, and before January 1, 2023. That percentage drops to 80% for property you buy in 2023, 60% for property you buy in 2024, 40% for property you buy in 2025, and 20% for property you buy in 2026. Generally, "qualified property" means anything except real estate and land improvements.

This may not sound like much after all that gobbledygook about basis, recovery periods, recovery methods, and conventions, but trust me when I say that this is a big deal.

It will make buying stuff for your business easier to afford and easier to account for.

Business Interest

Of course, what one hand gives, the other sometimes takes away. Traditionally, businesses have been able to write off an unlimited amount of interest they use to finance the assets we just talked about depreciating. You may have heard that the new law limits deductions for business interest. That's true – but those limits aren't likely to affect most of you:

- For starters, the limits don't apply unless your business averages $25 million or more in gross receipts.
- Even then, you can still deduct interest up to whatever amount of interest you earn, plus 30% of your adjusted taxable income, plus any floor-plan interest you pay to finance your stock.
- Finally, you can carry forward any disallowed interest deduction as long as you need.

Domestic Production Activities

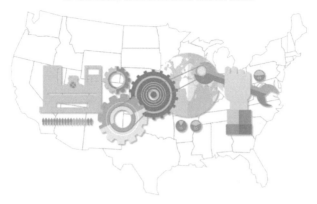

We've said before that Washington uses the tax code to do lots more than just raise revenue. One of those goals is encouraging manufacturing here in the United States, as opposed to overseas.

The American Jobs Creation Act of 2004 created the Domestic Production Activities Deduction (DPAD) to promote jobs in domestic manufacturing. The resulting Section 199 rules let businesses with "qualified production activities" deduct up to 9% of their net income from those activities. The rules are complicated, but the deductions can be substantial.

At least . . . the deductions *could* be substantial. I could go into more detail, but there's not much point because, as you probably guessed, the new law repeals that deduction.

Business Entertainment

Here's a change that most taxpayers aren't going to like. Under the old rules, you could deduct 50% of the cost of any entertainment expenses that took place directly before or after a substantial, bona fide discussion directly related to the active conduct of your business. Deductions included the face value of tickets to sporting and theatrical events, food and beverages, parking, taxes, and tips. The new law repeals that deduction, regardless of what business entity you operate.

The new law also tightens rules for deducting business meals. Previously, you could deduct 100% of the cost of providing food and beverages to your employees through an eating facility that qualified as "de minimis" fringe benefits. The new rule cuts that deduction to just 50%.

Fines and Penalties

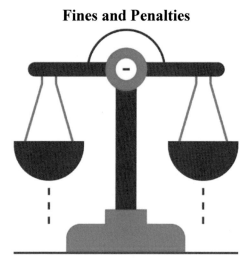

The new law also makes some changes to how businesses can treat fines and penalties.

First, it denies deductions for any settlement, payout, or attorney fees related to sexual harassment or sexual abuse if the settlement includes a nondisclosure agreement. Obviously, this is more of a messaging provision, in light of recent Congressional sexual harassment scandals, than a serious revenue-raiser.

It also loosens the general rule that fines or penalties are nondeductible by carving out an exception for amounts, identified as such in a court order or settlement agreement, as restitution, remediation, or required to come into compliance with any law.

Net Operating Losses

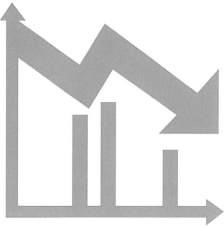

In an ideal world, your business would make money, year after year – and lots of it.

But we don't live in an ideal world, and sometimes businesses lose money. If a taxpayer – meaning, a C corporation or individual owner of a pass-through business – loses more money than it makes in a year, that loss is called a "net operating loss." And while nobody wants to lose money, a net operating loss doesn't just get wasted – it can help you save tax in a different year.

Under the old rules, if you had a net operating loss, you could carry it back for up to two years and get a refund, depending on the size of that loss, of up to 100% of the taxes you paid in those previous years. If the net operating loss was more than you made in those previous two years, you could carry it forward up to 20 years. Alternatively, you could elect to forego the carryback and just carry the losses forward. (This might make sense if you expected to be in a higher tax bracket going forward than you were in those past two years.)

The new law makes three changes to the NOL rules:

1. It eliminates the two-year carry*back* period, except for farming businesses and property/casualty insurance companies.
2. It lets you carry your unused NOLs forward indefinitely, rather than just 20 years.
3. Finally, it limits your NOL deduction for future years to 80% of that year's taxable income.

I realize that nobody likes to lose money. But NOLs can be the tax-planning equivalent of gold. Forget carrying them forward 20 years – if you have NOLs, we can help you make magic with them *now*.

NEW RULES FOR ESTATES

Benjamin Franklin once said the only certain things in life are death and taxes (smart guy, that Franklin), and that was *before* we had an estate tax! So let's talk about what happens after you file that final 1040 and go on to settle accounts with your Maker.

Estate Taxes

Under the old law, effective beginning in 2011, estates were subject to a 40% tax. However, there was a $5 million per person "unified credit," which effectively meant that only about two out of every thousand estates actually paid the tax.

That unified credit amount was also indexed for inflation, so by 2017, the threshold had grown to $5.49 million.

The easy solution to avoiding estate tax, if your net worth is above the threshold, might be to just give away enough of your assets before you die to avoid the tax. The IRS is way ahead of you here, which is why there's a gift tax. You could give up to a $15,000 "annual exclusion" amount to anyone you like, without any gift or estate tax consequence. If you're married, you and your spouse can make "split gifts" of up to $30,000 per person. There's also a gift tax unified credit, equal to the same amount as the estate tax credit. Once your total taxable lifetime gifts exceed that total, you start owing the actual tax at the same 40%.

So now it's time for some bad news and some good news.

The bad news is, the estate tax lives on. The House bill would have eliminated it entirely, for decedents dying after 2024. But that proposal just cost too much, so it didn't make the final cut.

The good news is, the new law doubles the unified credit – adjusted for inflation, it's now $11.2 million per person.

When was the last time you reviewed your estate plan? If you're like most people, the answer is "not recently enough." We run into countless business owners with outdated estate plans. And while it's always possible to update a stale *tax* plan, once you die, there's no chance to update a stale *estate* plan.

SURPRISE!

Are you one of those unhappy Americans looking at paying *more* under the new law? Here's some news that will help you drown your

Raise A Toast!

sorrows. The overall tax act incorporates the Craft Beverage Modernization and Tax Reform Act. So raise a toast to these new rules!

- The federal excise tax on beer drops from $18 to $16 on a brewer's first two million barrels. For brewers who produce less than that amount, the tax on the first 60,000 barrels drops from $7.50 to $3.00 per barrel. (That works about to a heady 4.3 cents per pint.)
- The law expands the excise tax credit for larger wineries, lets sparkling wines qualify, increases the alcohol-by-volume (ABV) qualifying for the $1.07 tax rate from 14% to 16%, and increases the carbonation allowed in certain low-alcohol wines.
- Finally, the law reduces the federal excise tax on distilled spirits, which currently stands at a flat $13.50 per gallon, to $2.70 each for their first 100,000 proof gallons, $13.34 for the next 22,030,000 gallons, and $13.50 for anything above that. (A proof gallon is one liquid gallon of spirits at 100 proof.)

Congressional Living Expenses

Here's a provision that might satisfy your sense of justice. Code Section 162 say that members of Congress can deduct up to $3,000 per year for living expenses while they're away from their districts.

Now, some members have made headlines for bunking on cots in their offices and showering at the Congressional gym. Others rent group houses on nearby Capitol Hill, living like overgrown frat brothers. (Years ago, Amazon broadcast a series called Alpha House about a group of republican senators sharing a house.) Those guys could probably use that $3,000 deduction.

But with most members of Congress having a seven-figure net worth, and congressional approval ratings hovering somewhere around 11%, this isn't the time for members to be rewarding themselves. (Besides, many commentators say, they're already doing that by lowering the tax on the income they used to get themselves elected to Congress in the first place!) So the new law eliminates that little boondoggle.

Ride Your Bike To Work

Ok, this one just seems petty and mean. Under the old law, you could exclude a whopping $20 per month for expenses related to riding your bike to work, so long as you weren't getting other pretax transit benefits. The new law kills that benefit. And how much will letting the air out of this break save the Treasury? Austin Powers fans, channel your best Dr. Evil voice and say it with me: *"one . . . million . . . dollars."* A whole million dollars a year in new revenue. A rounding error, at best. (By contrast, the bill keeps tax breaks for car commuters that cost the Treasury $8.6 *billion* per year.)

Obamacare "Repeal"

Here's a final provision you may have heard about the new law –
that it somehow "repeals" Obamacare. That's not actually true, despite
what your right-wing uncle says at your family Thanksgiving dinner.

One of Obamacare's central components is the "individual
mandate" – the requirement that every American carry health
insurance, or pay a penalty with their taxes. For 2017, that penalty is
$695 per adult and $347.50 per child, or 2.5% of your AGI, whichever
is higher.

The Tax Cuts and Jobs Act doesn't actually *repeal* the mandate. It
reduces that penalty to $0, beginning in 2019.

However, the new law doesn't repeal the employer mandate, the
exchanges, the new coverage and benefits requirements, or any of
Obamacare's other substantive healthcare provisions. It also doesn't
repeal Obamacare's 3.8% net investment income tax.

Tax On College Endowments

Colleges and universities have traditionally taken gifts from alumni, parents, and other supporters, and used them to build endowments to generate income to build and maintain facilities, hire faculty and staff, and discount tuition for needy students. Schools generally qualify as nonprofit charities, so there's no tax on their earnings – at least, not until now.

The new law imposes a 1.4% tax on earnings from the very richest schools – private schools with over 500 students and endowments over $500,000 per student. It should affect only a few dozen schools – Ivy League names like Harvard and Princeton, along with "Little Ivies" like Amherst, Bowdoin, and Hamilton. And the tax itself is only expected to raise about $1.8 billion over the next 10 years.

At first glance, the new tax looks like more of a rounding error than a real threat. Princeton University's endowment is $22.2 billion, which works out to $2.5 million per student. If the fund earns 8% per year, that 1.4% rate works out to just under $25 million in tax. But that's over $3,000 per student, which is significant. Right now, Princeton uses that endowment to admit students without considering whether they can afford it or not. Students from families earning under $65,000 pay no tuition, room, or board. 82% of Princeton students graduate debt-free, and the average debt for those who do borrow is just $8,900.

So, *somebody* is going to lose out because of the tax. And Princeton's endowment per student is the highest in the country, with five times the amount per student as the threshold of the tax. Who knows what effect it will have on schools without the same resources?

Alaska National Wildlife Refuge

Here's a provision that has absolutely nothing to do with taxes – at least, not directly.

The Alaska National Wildlife Refuge (ANWR) includes 19.2 million acres in the far northeast corner of Alaska, partially bordering Ivvavik National Park in Canada's Yukon Territory. To call it "remote" would be an understatement – the nearest "cities" are Barrow, home to about 3,000 hardy souls, and Kaktovik, population 258. But ANWR is also home to more plant and animal species than any other protected area in the Arctic Circle, with six different ecozones spanning 200 miles north to south. Animal residents include over 100,000 caribou, moose, musk oxen, Canadian lynxes, bears, wolves, and birds.

In 1977, Washington banned drilling for oil in the area. But ever since then, energy industry forces have worked to allow it in a 1.5 million-acre subsection of coastline known as the "1002 area." The Tax Cuts and Jobs Act directs the Department of the Interior, which currently manages ANWR, to hold lease sales in 1002 area, which they estimate contains 11.8 billion barrels of technically recoverable crude oil.

Alaska Senator Lisa Murkowski, who has worked for years to open ANWR to drilling, reports that surface development will be limited to just 2,000 acres. And the law doesn't mean that drilling will start any time soon – there will be lots of scrutiny, lots of permit reviews, and plenty of lawsuits, too. It may be a decade before drilling actually starts, if ever. But the new law at least opens the door to that possibility.

Benched Proposals

Finally, let's finish with some scary proposals that *didn't* make the final cut.

The German Chancellor Otto von Bismarck once famously said that "laws are like sausages, it is better not to see them being made." That's sound advice – and it's just as true for the Tax Cuts and Jobs Act of 2017 as it is for any other major legislation.

The House of Representatives introduced their version of the bill on November 2, 2017. They passed it on November 16. The Senate passed their version shortly after midnight on December 2. As is generally the case when the House and Senate pass differing versions of the same bill, each side appointed members to meet in conference to reconcile their efforts and craft a single bill acceptable to both houses. That bill passed the House on December 19 and the Senate on December 20; the President signed it on December 22.

That's awfully fast passage for such important legislation. (The Tax Reform Act of 1986, took nearly two years to hopscotch its way through Congress before passing.) It's even faster considering how many proposals the House and Senate considered and in some cases adopted before crafting the final bill.

Many of these proposals made headlines when they first hit rumor mills, or even passed one or both houses of Congress. However, in the end, none of them made the final grade:

- Current law lets you exclude up to $250,000 of capital gains from the sale of your home ($500,000 for joint filers), so long as you own it and occupy it as your primary residence for two of the previous five years. The House and Senate both proposed to tighten these periods to five of the previous eight years. In fact, the House bill would have gone even further and phased out the exclusion as your income went up. Fortunately, for most of us at least, neither proposal made it to the final bill.

- The House bill would have repealed the deduction for student loan interest.

- The House bill would have repealed the deduction for employer-provided adoption assistance.

- The House bill would have repealed the $7,500 electric vehicle credit.

- The House bill originally proposed to eliminate dependent care flexible spending accounts immediately. Then it proposed to wait until 2023 to drop the hammer. The final bill leaves those accounts intact.

- The House bill would have taxed graduate students and other employees of educational institutions who receive discounted or free tuition or waivers for themselves, their spouses, or their dependents. This could have absolutely decimated grad school enrollments, with students owing up to $10,000 or more in taxes on their scholarships.

- Both houses were rumored to be considering lowering the deduction for 401(k) contributions.

- The House bill would have eliminated the $250 deduction for educator expenses, the classroom supplies that teachers cover out of their own, richly-compensated pockets. The Senate bill would have doubled it. Neither provision made it to the final bill. (Talk about splitting the difference!)

- Under current law, when you sell stock or mutual funds from a taxable investment account, and you have different shares with different costs, you can specify which shares you're selling in order to minimize your tax. (Generally this means selling the highest-cost shares first.) The Senate bill would have required you to sell the oldest shares first, regardless of price. Once again, that provision never made it into the final bill.

- The Senate bill would have expanded Section 529 accounts for use with private and parochial K-12 tuition and homeschooling expenses.

- For years now, a motley coalition of foes (including even President Trump) have attacked the so-called "carried interest" loophole, which lets private equity and hedge fund managers pay tax on their generally supersized income at preferential capital gains rates. The new law keeps those rates, although it imposes a three-year holding period (rather than the current one). Fund managers may even qualify for the new Qualified Business Income deduction.

HAVE YOU MISSED THESE?

By now it should be clear that the Tax Cuts and Jobs Act offers lots of planning opportunities, especially for business owners. The new Qualified Business Income rules alone should be enough to keep an army of tax lawyers busy for years.

Have I convinced you that now is a great time to sit down for Strategic Tax Planning? Good!

But planning has always offered you the opportunity to pay less. And if you're like most business owners, you've never sat down to plan. And that could be costing you big time, even *before* the new rules. So now let's take a look at some of the classic Strategic Tax Planning strategies that you may have missed in the past.

Too Much Self-Employment Tax

If you operate your business as a sole proprietorship (or a single-member LLC taxed as a sole proprietorship), you may pay as much in self-employment tax as you do in income tax. If that's the case, you might consider setting up an S corporation to reduce that tax.

If you're taxed as a sole proprietor, you'll report your net income on Schedule C. You'll pay tax at whatever your personal rate is. But you'll also pay self-employment tax, of 15.3% on "net self-employment income" up to the Social Security "wage base" ($128,400 for 2018) and 2.9% of anything above that. You're also subject to a 0.9% Medicare surtax on anything above $200,000 if you're single, $250,000 if you're married filing jointly, or $125,000 if you're married filing separately.

Sole Proprietorship

Report net income on Schedule C

Pay *income* tax on net income

Pay *SE* tax up to 15.3% on income

Let's say your profit at the end of the year is $80,000.
You'll pay regular tax at your regular rate, whatever that is.

You'll also pay about $11,000 in self-employment tax.

That self-employment tax replaces the Social Security and Medicare tax that your employer would pay and withhold if you weren't self-employed. If you're like most readers, you're not planning to retire on that Social Security. You'll be delighted if it's all still there, but you're not actually counting on it in any meaningful way.

What if there was a way you could take part of that Social Security contribution and invest it yourself? Do you think you could earn more on your money yourself than you can with the Social Security Administration? Well, there is, and it's called an S corporation.

S-Corporation

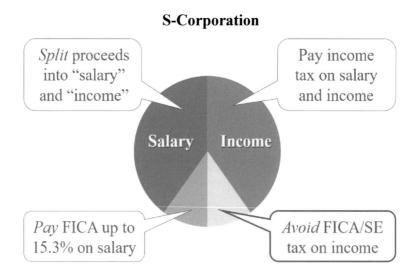

Split proceeds into "salary" and "income"

Pay income tax on salary and income

Salary · Income

Pay FICA up to 15.3% on salary

Avoid FICA/SE tax on income

An S corporation is a special corporation that's taxed somewhat like a partnership. The corporation pays you a salary for the work you do. Then, if there's any profit left over, it passes the profit through to your personal return, and you pay the tax on that income on your own return. The S corporation splits your income into two parts, wages and pass-through distributions.

Here's why the S corporation is so attractive.

You'll pay the same 15.3% employment tax on your wages as you would on your self-employment income. (You'll also pay the extra 0.9% Medicare tax on self-employment income exceeding $200,000 or $250,000, depending on whether you file alone or jointly.)

BUT – there's no Social Security or self-employment tax due on the dividend pass-through. And that makes a world of difference.

Employment Tax Comparison

S-Corp FICA		Proprietorship SE	
Salary	$40,000	Income	$80,000
FICA	$6,120	SE Tax	$11,304
Net	$73,880	Net	$68,696

S-Corp *Saves*
$5,184

Let's say your S corporation earns the same $80,000 as your proprietorship. If you pay yourself $40,000 in wages, you'll pay about $6,120 in Social Security.

But you'll *avoid* employment tax on the income distribution.

And *that* saves you $5,184 in employment tax you would have paid without the S-corporation.

The best part here is that you just pay less tax. It's not like buying equipment at the end of the year to get big depreciation deductions. That may be a great strategy, but it also means spending something on the equipment to get that depreciation. It's not like contributing money to a retirement plan to get deductions. That may be another great strategy, but it also means you must take money out of your budget to contribute to the plan.

Now, you still must pay yourself a "reasonable salary" for the service you provide as an employee – in other words, the salary you would have to pay to hire an employee to do the work for you. If you pay yourself nothing, or merely a token amount, the IRS can recharacterize up to *all of* your income as wage and hit you with some very hefty taxes, interest, and penalties. So don't get greedy! But according to IRS data, the average S corporation pays out about 40% of its income in the form of salary and 60% in the form of distributions. You can see that there's at least a possibility for real savings.

Missing Medical Expenses

Now let's talk about health-care costs. Surveys used to show that taxes *used* to be small business owners' biggest concern. Now it's rising health care costs.

If you pay for your own health insurance, you can deduct it as an adjustment to income on Page 1 of Form 1040. If you itemize deductions, you can deduct unreimbursed medical and dental expenses on Schedule A, *if* they total more than 10% of your adjusted gross income. But most of us just don't spend that much on our healthcare. So, we wind up losing thousands in otherwise legitimate deductions.

What if there was a way to write off medical bills as business expenses? There is, and it's called a Medical Expense Reimbursement Plan, or Section 105 Plan.

"Employee" Benefit Plan

Sole Proprietorship	• Hire Spouse
Partnership	• Hire Spouse (if < 5% owner)
C-Corporation	• Hire Self
S-Corporation	• > 2% Shareholders/Spouse Ineligible

The first thing you need to know about a MERP is that it's an *employee* benefit plan. That means (spoiler alert) it requires an employee:

- If your business is taxed as a sole proprietorship, you're considered self-employed. You can't establish the plan for yourself. However, if you're married, you can hire your spouse.
- If your business is taxed as a partnership, you're also considered self-employed. Again, you can't establish the plan for yourself. However, you can still hire your spouse so long as he or she owns less than 5% of the business.
- If your business is taxed as an S corporation, both you and your spouse are considered self-employed. This means you'll need another source of income, not taxed as an S corporation, to establish the plan. (Alternatively, you can establish a health savings account, which we'll discuss in a few pages, to give

yourself most of the same benefit as the 105 plan.)

- If your business is taxed as a "C" corporation, you qualify as your own employee, so you can simply hire yourself.

If you're married, and you choose to hire your spouse, you don't even have to pay him or her a salary. You can compensate them in the form of benefits only, which avoids the hassle of filing payroll returns. The main requirement here is that the benefits you pay have to be "reasonable compensation" for the service they perform. If your spouse works an hour a month filing invoices for you, you'll probably have a hard time convincing an auditor that that's "reasonable" for $4,000 worth of LASIK surgery!

Eligible Expenses
- Major medical, LTC, Medicare, "Medigap" insurance
- Co-pays, deductibles, prescriptions
- Dental, vision, and chiropractic
- Braces, LASIK, fertility, special schools
- OTC medications (by prescription)

Once the plan is in place, you can reimburse your employee for any medical expense they incur for themselves, their spouse, and their dependents.

- This includes any kind of health insurance, including major medical, long-term care (up to specific IRS limits), Medicare premiums, and even Medigap coverage.

- It includes all your copays, deductibles, "co-insurance,' and other amounts insurance doesn't pay.
- It includes all your prescription drugs.
- It includes expenses for things like dental care, vision care, and chiropractic care that traditional insurance might not cover.
- It includes some really "big-ticket" items like braces for your kids' teeth, fertility treatments, and special schools for learning-disabled children. Let's say your physician diagnoses your 8-year-old son with ADHD, and prescribes *tai kwon do* lessons. Guess what – those lessons are now tax-deductible!
- It even includes over-the-counter medications and supplies, so long as they're actually prescribed by a physician.

One big advantage of the MERP is that it works with any insurance policy. You don't have to buy special coverage. You can use a MERP with insurance you buy on your own or insurance you buy through an exchange. If your spouse gets coverage from their employer, you can even set up a MERP in your business to cover whatever out-of-pocket expenses your spouse's insurance doesn't cover.

Let's assume you're a sole proprietor with two kids and you've hired your husband to work for your business. The plan lets you reimburse your husband/employee for all medical and dental expenses he incurs for himself – his spouse (which brings you into the plan) – and his dependents, the kids.

This includes all those expenses listed above.

The best part is, this is money you'd spend anyway, whether you got a deduction or not. You'll spend your money on glasses or your kids' braces whether it's deductible or not. The MERP just lets you move it from someplace on your return where you certainly can't deduct all of it (and probably can't deduct *any* of it), to a place where you can.

The Paperwork
- Written plan document
- Benefits = "reasonable compensation"
- Documents payments
- Certification
- PCORI fee

Okay, how do you make it work? Well, for starters, you'll need a written plan document.

If you've hired your spouse, you'll need to be able to verify that they qualify as a bona fide "employee." That means you need to direct the work they perform for the business, the same as you would direct the work that any other employee performs.

Here's one important requirement that the IRS *will* pay attention to in the unlikely event you get audited. You *do* have to run the payments through the actual business. You can't just pay medical bills out of the family personal account, total them up at the end of the year, and throw them on the business return.

This means you have two choices. You can pay health-care providers directly out of the business account. Or you can reimburse your employees for expenses they pay out of their personal funds. Let's say your husband needs to pick up a prescription. He can use his own money, and you can reimburse him. Or he can use a business credit card and charge it to the business directly.

There's generally no need for an outside third-party administrator, or "TPA," if you've simply hired your spouse to write off your own family's medical expenses. However, you will need a TPA if you're reimbursing nonfamily employees in order to avoid violating medical privacy rules.

There's no pre-funding required. You don't have to open a special bank or investment account, like with Health Savings Accounts or flex-spending plans. You don't have to decide up front how much you want to contribute to the plan, like you do with flexible spending accounts, and there's no "use it or lose it" rule. The MERP is really just an accounting device that lets you recharacterize your family medical bills as a business expense.

The MERP doesn't just help you save income tax. It also helps you save *self-employment* tax. Remember, when you work for yourself, you pay a special self-employment tax, which replaces the Social Security and Medicare taxes that you and your employer would share on your salary. That self-employment tax is based on your "net self-employment earnings" – but when you set up a MERP, the deduction reduces that self-employment income.

MERP Requirements
- Must cover "eligible employees"
- Exclusions
  - Under age 25
  - Under 35 hours/week
  - Under 9 months/year
  - Under 3 years' service
  - Collective bargaining agreement
- Excise tax on Form 720

Now, here's the bad news. If you have non-family employees, you have to include them too. Now, you can exclude employees under age 25, who work less than 35 hours per week, less than nine months per year, or who have worked for you less than three years. You can also exclude employees covered by a collective bargaining agreement that includes health benefits. But still, having non-family employees may make it too expensive to reimburse everyone as generously as you'd cover your own family.

Obamacare also imposes a pesky new excise tax requirement on MERPs called the "Patient Centered Outcomes Research Trust Fund Fee," or PCORI fee. For plans operating in 2017, that amount was $2.39 per person, reported on IRS Form 720, and due by July 31, 2019.

Yes, you heard that right. $2.39. You can't even buy a decent cup of coffee for that much. But the statutory penalty for failing to file that report can be as high as $10,000. And while it's not likely the IRS will ever actually impose that fine, you probably want to make sure you dot your "i's" and cross your "t's."

Health Savings Accounts

If a Medical Expense Reimbursement Plan isn't appropriate – either because you don't have a spouse to hire, or you have non-family employees you would have to cover – consider establishing a Health Savings Account. These arrangements combine a high-deductible health plan with a tax-free savings account to cover unreimbursed costs.

High Deductible Health Plan
- $1,300+ deductible (individual coverage)
- $2,600+ deductible (family coverage)

Health Savings Account
- Contribute & deduct up to $3,450/$6,900 per year
- Account grows tax-free
- Tax-free withdrawals for qualified expenses

To qualify, you'll need to be covered by a "high deductible health plan." This means the deductible is at least $1,300 for single coverage or $2,600 for family coverage. Neither you nor your spouse can be covered by a "*non*-high deductible health plan" or by Medicare. The plan can't cover any expense, other than certain preventive care benefits, until you satisfy the annual deductible. You're not eligible if you're covered by a separate plan or rider offering prescription drug benefits before the minimum annual deductible is satisfied.

Once you've established your eligibility, you can open a deductible "health savings account" to cover out-of-pocket expenses not covered by your insurance. For 2017, you can contribute up to $3,450 if you have individual coverage or $6,900 if you have family coverage. (If you're 55 or older, you can save an extra $1,000 per year.)

HSAs are easy to open. Most banks, brokerage firms, and insurance companies offer them. Many times you can even get a debit card to charge expenses directly to the account.

Once you're up and running, you can use your account for most kinds of health insurance, including COBRA continuation and long-term care (but not "Medigap" coverage). You can also use it for the same sort of expenses as a MERP – copays, deductibles, prescriptions, and other out-of-pocket costs.

Withdrawals are tax-free so long as you use them for "qualified medical costs." Withdrawals *not* used for qualified medical costs are subject to regular income tax plus a 20% penalty.

After your death, your account passes to your specified beneficiary. If your beneficiary is your spouse, they can treat it as their own HSA. If not, your beneficiary will pay ordinary tax on the account proceeds (but not the 20% penalty).

The Health Savings Account isn't quite as powerful or flexible as the MERP. You've got specific dollar limits on what you can contribute to the account, which might not match your out-of-pocket costs. And there's no self-employment tax advantage as there is with a MERP. But Health Savings Accounts can still help cut your overall health-care costs by giving you bigger tax deductions.

Rent Your House to Yourself

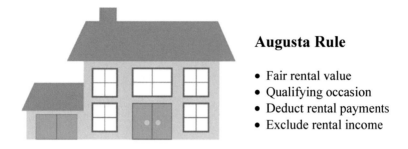

Augusta Rule

- Fair rental value
- Qualifying occasion
- Deduct rental payments
- Exclude rental income

Here's a fun deduction your tax professional probably never told you about, and might not even know about. You can rent your house to yourself to create tax-free income!

Section 280A(g) of the Internal Revenue Code lets you rent out your home for up to 14 days per year without even having to report the income.

This is sometimes called the "Augusta Rule" in honor of the residents of Augusta, Georgia, who rent their homes to spectators visiting to attend the annual Masters golf tournament. You'll also see residents of Super Bowl host cities, political convention sites, music festivals, and Olympic Games host cities take advantage of the rule. And many taxpayers who live in less exotic locations take advantage of the opportunity to rent out their vacation homes when they would otherwise sit empty.

However, this rule also opens the door to renting your home to your business, paying a *reasonable* deductible rent out of the business account, and then treating it as non-taxable income when it hits your personal account. You can rent your home for all sorts of purposes, including business meetings, employee events, and even a limited amount of employee entertainment.

The key to making this work is to document your *bona fide* use of the home, and show that the rent you charge is reasonable:

- To document your business use, keep records indicating who attended the event, and your business relationship with them. If you use the home for meetings, keep minutes or other records of the business discussion that takes place at the home.
- To document "reasonable" rent, get quotes from hotels, country clubs, or similar venues for use of their meeting facilities. Alternatively, you could research rates from similar properties on Airbnb or similar sites. Or you could take a percentage of your home's rental value as reported on Zillow.com.

Example: You schedule a meeting of your corporation's Board of Directors at your home. You check into fees at local hotels and business clubs, and determine the daily rent for a comparable space is $500. Your corporation writes you a check for $500 and deducts it as "rent" on its annual return. You deposit that check into your personal account, but you don't need to report it as income on your personal return.

But Wait . . . There's More!

The S corporation to save employment tax, the MERP, and the Augusta Rule are all tried-and-true strategies that proper planning can help you unlock. And they have *nothing* to do with the new tax law.

But, as the late-night infomercials say . . . there's more!

Did you know you may be able to deduct your backyard swimming pool as an "on-premises employee athletic facility?"

Do you know how to write off summer barbecues and other meals you serve at home?

Did you know how that standard 54.5 cents/mile allowance for business use of your car could be costing you big-time?

Do you know which qualified retirement plan choice makes the best sense for your business? Do you know if you should even be sponsoring a qualified plan at all?

Do you know how to allocate your retirement savings between taxable, tax-deferred, and nontaxable assets?

Do you know how to find the most tax-efficient money managers for your portfolio? (No, it's not the mutual fund the friendly guy in your foursome says you should buy.)

Do you know the three ways that supposedly "tax-free" municipal bonds can actually cost you taxes?

Do you know about charitable planning strategies that can pay for themselves even if you're not already charitably inclined?

Do you know the family tax-planning strategy that lets you take fully-depreciated business equipment and other property and essentially "depreciate" it all over again?

Again, these are all tried-and-true strategies that you may have simply missed in the past. So, while planning now makes sense to take advantage of the new laws, you shouldn't miss out on any of the opportunities that have always been there waiting for you!

WHERE DO WE GO FROM HERE?

Now that you understand how the new tax law works, at least from 30,000 feet, let's talk about **where to go from here.**

You saw, when we looked at our case studies, how much the new law may save you all by itself. But there are a lot of moving parts, especially for business owners. And there are a lot of opportunities you have to plan for to take advantage of.

That's where we come in. We offer true, proactive Strategic Tax Planning to help you make the most of the new tax law, and catch up on opportunities you may have missed under existing law, too.

The process works like going to the doctor. If you're sick, the doctor starts with a diagnosis: what's causing the pain? Then he prescribes a solution – maybe it's a prescription, or surgery, or physical therapy. Finally, someone fills that prescription.

We work the same way. We start by sitting down with you for a free Tax Analysis where we review your returns to find the mistakes and missed opportunities that may be costing you thousands in taxes you don't have to pay.

"If you don't have a Tax Blueprint®, you really don't have a tax plan at all."

Then we prescribe the solutions to stop that bleeding. That prescription is called a **Tax Blueprint®**, and Financial Gravity is the *only* place where you can get it. If you don't have a Tax Blueprint®, you really don't have a tax plan at all.

Finally, we'll fill those prescriptions. Here at Financial Gravity, we call that a **Tax Operating System®**. In some cases, we'll do it ourselves. In others, we'll bring in a network of specialty vendors who offer services like cost segregation studies, captive insurance management, or charitable trust administration.

We can't tell you how much we can save until we sit down with you for the analysis. However, we can tell you that most business owners are wasting tens-to-hundreds of thousands of dollars a year in taxes they simply didn't know they didn't have to pay. And that was true even *before* the new law! The Tax Cuts and Jobs Act of 2017 just gives us *more* opportunities to cut your bill.

> **"most business owners are wasting tens-to-hundreds of thousands of dollars a year in taxes"**

You owe it to yourself to make sure you're making the most of every opportunity, under the old laws *and* the new. **So pick up the phone and call us now!**

FINANCIAL®
GRAVITY
lower taxes • higher profit • greater wealth

469-342-9100
www.financialgravity.com

For the very latest regarding the Tax Cuts and Jobs Act and updates to this book, please visit:
www.thenewtaxlawbook.com

ABOUT THE AUTHOR

Ed Lyon is a graduate of Hamilton College and the University of Cincinnati College of Law, where he served as executive Editor of the University of Cincinnati Law Review.

Ed began his career as a staff aide to Representatives Jack Kemp and Dick Cheney. He has written and edited tax-oriented publications for The National Underwriter Company, advised clients as a Financial Consultant for Merrill Lynch, and developed his own planning-based practice specializing in real estate agents and investors.

Ed is the creator of the TaxCoach software planning system, where he has helped thousands of accountants and financial advisors use proactive Strategic Tax Planning to develop their practices. He serves today as Chief Tax Strategist for TaxCoach Software and Financial Gravity Companies, Inc., a Dallas-based provider of Fractional Family Office® services.

Ed has delivered over 300 live presentations and 500 radio and television broadcasts, including appearances on CNN, Fox News, MSNBC, CNBC, and even Roseanne Barr's short-lived talk show, where she dubbed him "the funniest tax guy in America."

OTHER BOOKS BY ED LYON

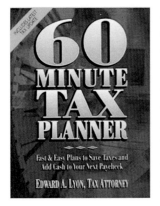

How to save time and money on your taxes--a simple, do-it-yourself tax cutting guide. Finally, a book that takes the fear--and loathing--out of tax time. Because unlike other books on the market that focus solely on tax preparation, the *60 Minute Tax Planner* is the ultimate guide to tax savings. Using a simple question-and-answer style, it helps readers navigate the mind-bogglingly complex provisions of the federal tax code to calculate exactly how much they can save on their income tax bill. What's more, this total "tax tuneup" doesn't waste time. It's designed to let readers zero in immediately on their own important target areas such as investments, employment, retirement, and filing returns. Handy worksheets and checklists make it easy to start putting more cash back into that paycheck right away. With its take-charge prescription for lower taxes in less time, the *60 Minute Tax Planner* is a lifeline for those who prepare their own returns and an excellent preparation tool for others who hire professional tax advisers.

Paying tax bites. The *Investors Tax Tuneup* helps you bite book. The book is full of sound strategies for making more, and keeping more, from your investments. Learn how to choose stocks, bonds, and mutual funds. Take advantage of qualified plans, IRAs, life insurance, and annuities. Avoid tax on your capital gains. This is a concise, easy-to-understand guide from a nationally recognized expert who's been called "the funniest tax guy in America."

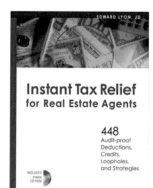

Now, South-Western Publishing brings you Ed's plain-English guide to keeping your money. Ed Lyon's *Instant Tax Relief for Real Estate Agents* offers six easy-to-understand sections outlining how the tax system works, what you need to know about starting your business, tax strategies for buying residential and commercial property, and the most comprehensive list of deductions, credits, loopholes, and strategies for agents anywhere. Special planning guides, filing guides, "land mines," and Internet guides flesh out these strategies and give you the tools to help you plan and prepare your financial future.

MY ACTION PLAN TO KEEP MORE OF WHAT I MAKE

_____

_____

_____

_____

_____

_____

_____

_____

_____

_____

_____

_____

_____

_____

_____

_____

_____

_____

_____

_____

_____

_____

_____

_____

_____

82710797R00062

Made in the USA
Middletown, DE
05 August 2018